sulphurtongue

CHAPBOOKS BY REBECCA SALAZAR

the knife you need to justify the wound

Guzzle

sulphurtongue

REBECCA SALAZAR

McClelland & Stewart

McClelland & Stewart and colophon are registered trademarks of Penguin Random House
Canada Limited.

Grateful acknowledgement is made to reprint the following previously published material:
Leslie Jamison, excerpts from "The Empathy Exams" from The Empathy Exams: Essays.
Copyright © 2014 by Leslie Jamison. Reprinted with the permission of The Permissions
Company, LLC on behalf of Graywolf Press, www.graywolfpress.org. Kim Hyesoon, as
translated by Don Mee Choi, excerpts from "Morning Greetings" from Sorrowtoothpaste
Mirrorcream. Copyright © 2014 by Kim Hyesoon. Reprinted with the permission of
Action Books, www.actionbooks.org.

Published simultaneously in the United States of America.

Library and Archives Canada Cataloguing in Publication data is available upon request.

ISBN: 978-0-7710-9469-9
ebook ISBN: 978-0-7710-9470-5

Book design by Kate Sinclair
Cover images: (azaleas) Branch of Azaleas in Bloom by M. de Gijselaar (1831). Original from
The Rijksmuseum. Digitally enhanced by rawpixel.; (spiders) Illustrated by Charles Dessalines
D' Orbigny (1806-1876). Digitally enhanced by rawpixel from a 1892 edition of Dictionnaire
Universel D'histoire Naturelle.

Typeset in Columbus by M&S, Toronto

Printed and bound in Canada

McClelland & Stewart,
a division of Penguin Random House Canada Limited,
a Penguin Random House Company
www.penguinrandomhouse.ca

1 2 3 4 5   25 24 23 22 21

CONTENTS

how to lose

femme phobias

doppelbanger

sulphur bonds

I have praised your God
For the blessing of the body, snuck
From pleasure to pleasure, lying for it,

—TRACY K. SMITH, FROM "INTERROGATIVE" IN *Duende*

how to lose

SYNAESTHESIA

Your name, pronounced,
feels stark against your teeth
like cold and cloves.

A paper-cut's smell is the way the knife nicks
a half-ripe peach pit.
It tastes the way it feels to dig a nail
into a maple's wet green seed
peeled slowly from its husk.

The body knows
that being pinched on the neck or the wrist
tastes like landing on your tailbone
after falling down the stairs,
and knows the colour of the cry
that surges crackling up your spine
is not the colour of the hardwood floor,
but is like that word, hardwood:
shiny, dark,
with fire
smothered in the gloss.

you and the sack of flour
and the fitful scents of hot dust, blood, and eucalyptus leaves
                        are all I know I come from.
                        and it could be just a story, that
you hide under a dead man for two days,
hearing the guns pass every hour on the street.
and you watch the smudge of flour
on the dead man's sleeve and are reminded
of your wife, the floured imprint of her hands
on her skirt as she is rolling out arepas,
like those days ago when there was not enough
to feed yourselves, your children,
                        or this future in which
                        I cobble genealogies
                        that falter in your line.
                        there is no proof that
when the streets fall dark and quiet
you shift the dead man's body from your back.
you place your hand across his cheek to close his mouth,
turn him away so you will never know his face.
                        there is no record of the way
your sack of flour exhales a fine, white breath
that lingers, coiling slowly in the flicker of a street lamp,
as you hoist with your wait-stiff arms,
                        nor of the way that
days of shouldering a punctured body
make the flour a weightless burden, now,
to carry: heavy only with the scent of your own warmth
and with the spent breeze of humid night.
                        but the name of the street
                        and the shape of the ditch where you've lain
                        are the shapes of the slow benign marks on my chest,

and the name of the man you held close
is a prayer in a language I've lost.
there are other men, face-down, lining each street
as you come home. you hear the guns call somewhere
and your front door opens hesitant, then blossoms like a wound.
I am pressing your dark, floured hand
when your family carries you in, shuts the door.
when your children hear your voice again
and rush to hold you
I dissolve
against their arms

1. (noun).
CGI favelas are superimposed
on the intricately lit sheen
of Zoe Saldana's left tricep
as she nuzzles a handgun between
praying hands, barrel kissing her brow
as the tasteful taupe words haloed
over her head decree Vengeance
Is Beautiful.

2. (verb).
The act of engaging in a rare form
of pica, during which the afflicted scarfs
national flags; she then regurgitates
them, fairy-godmothered
into the stars and the stripes
which will flutter aloft in Hi-Def,
lambent with traces of saliva.

3.a. (mistake).
Yours, North America,
for schools that flagrantly neglect
to teach all pupils all the finer points
of colonial-favela-parkour.
Your daughters cannot hack
the flexor tendons of unwelcome strangers
in point-oh-eight seconds.
Your nine-year-olds' tibias
still shatter at the mere sight
of repeated ten-foot falls.

6. (champagne).
Specifically, the Champagne
of Sodas, surreptitiously
containing a first taste
of Coors Light, siphoned into a glass
by *that* cousin, sniggering over the film
at the younger kids, because a girl
that age can't take it straight.

13.b. (mistake).
My father's, who marshalled
the video store run for the family reunion,
who too jauntily had all the kids
stack up like VHS tapes in the basement
to evangelize hope for our salvaged fate:
today, mis chinos,
you will learn about your country
from this lustrous DVD.

24. (synonym).
For "exotic,"
or "hot-tempered,"
or "hot-bodied,"
because Mexico, the usual booty call,
is getting quite bad press of late,
what with the actual Mexicans
splashed grossly across the newsways,
and let us not mention the wall.

8. (adjective).
The *L.A. Times* defines aptly
this B-movie blast
of bloody blam blam—
check your fingers and toes
for little traces of her blood,
listen close to that heart, beating:
Define. Define. Define.

11. (constellation).
In the quadrant Sagittarius;
all Third World Country movie sets
are mocked up from a blueprint
of the pattern in this cluster, in which
the stars spell out a woman's sharpened breasts
and sleek, protruding ribs,
rubbed with a coffee marinade,
garnished with rare, edible orchids.

i. Spanish

perro—dog, a word brief
and galumphing, puggish
growl of the double *r*,
quick, but large-pawed,
with the stem of the *p*
wagging into the next line of text.

pero—a tug on the leash
of negation, a less guttural way
to pull hard on a sentence, to give it
something new to chew on.

ii. English

but—your ears twitch
at the difference in pitch.
but for its roughness,
you've sniffed out a translation,
but found this word's sound
is a floppy-lipped whistle
you really can't roll with.

butt—the double consonant
no playful purr; now it's a crass tisk
like cigarette ends flicked
to seep ochre spittle on sidewalks.
hardly fetching, when the rhetoric
bounds out akin to first-grade
jokes: the crude titch of
"guess what? chicken butt!"
is less talking dog,
more spelling-bee semantics.

I should admit I would prefer the ghosts
come out fully screaming just to prove
that they are there; that I'm as likely
to turn up fucking wasted at your door
as I am to sprout long, verdant wings.
A haunting is only a pheromone stain,
the rate of cortisol secreted in a place
by bodies flown by fly-wings, wormed
to imperceptibility before you came.

I am the last resort my ancestors prayed
long they would not come to. Inconvenient
excess of emotion and of stubborn hair
with one foot slipping on banana peels
and one foot firmly in the grave. Loose end
to their long plait of generations—
guilty, although unrepentant, cup of flesh.

scribble the line from your name to your mother's
to find whatever accident that nose came from,
ancestral break that carved your crooked outlook.

water down the ink that spells your mother's name
since at her wedding, brothers tossed her frilled form
in the fountain square. wet the line that links her

to her mother, for the way abuela mourned the ruined
wedding dress, its bloated, chlorinated seams.
centre-justify the section where your uncles

christen their eighteen children with the same
six names, since symmetry is key for architects.
a blank space for your mother's father's mother

who abandoned him at twelve, leaving no semblance
of herself in him. he would not recognize her, either,
in the seventeen of her twenty-three siblings still living

when he found them. make your strongest line to join
his abuela, barefoot mender of the earth, who lay down
aged one hundred and twelve after hiking the finca at dawn

to repair a spent fence. a bristly golden line exalts
abuelo's father, patriarch whose name translates
to *lion lion lion*. fold paper houses for the cousins

in aracataca, shelter for the stories of their neighbour's
surly, bush-browed son who renamed home, discovered ice.
an ornate line rejoins abuela's uncle with the sun-black skin

and green eyes, still the envy of the few who even now
recall his beauty, but forget his name. a tenuous line
for a brother who drifted so far south he never called to say

he had a daughter. his sister's childless line bears
silhouettes of mountains she was not allowed to climb
when she, young socialist, was cloistered by her mother,

fearful she would follow bandolero ancestors, their secret
danger. pinprick thick constellations for abuelo's first sister,
her forty grandchildren—one for each day of the flood,

then, multiply to count their children, those who ebb
and flow in number with the moon. a shroud of volcanic ash
near the left margin, close to abuelo's abuela. fertile ground

once called armero, now fleshed with your once-kin, all buried
under fire. this line burns out.

list the cousins you grew with in foreign soil, and dig
to make room for their children, who burst like clustered
mushrooms past the bottom of the page. add a footnote

for the secret queers whose progeny are uncontainable
in lineage, biology, or text. ungenerative archivist,
you join them childless, not ungrateful. braced

with generations of accumulated love. you'll tend
a lurid garden in the margin. you'll feed this family
by composting this page into rich loam.

What if we don't come home in time
What if we don't come home tonight
What if we don't come home
What if we don't come home because we've died
      our families will have to come and tidy
      it would smell
What if we come and there's no home
What if we come and there's no home after the fire
What if there never was a home
What if we failed at that

you will watch the leaves
grow cigarette burns in late
fall. down your young body,
tar spot where the cankers

grow. cigarette burns lately
riddle your body with pitch,
tar. spot where the cankers
ache beyond their unsolved

riddle. your body will pitch,
fall down. you're young, body
aching but not beyond salve.
i will not watch you leave.

A DEATH PRECEDED BY THREE AUGURIES

i.

In your last week, when they say you might stop eating, you eat
twenty-seven watermelons whole. The brothers ogle:
pink juice parsing the lines of your face and depositing
carbuncles, sugar gems down your cracked lips and chin,
like the starched stars that web across summer fruit rinds.

ii.

The hospice halls heavy and cloying with jasmine and rose.
We are immersed. After lights-out, the sisters sneak
from the guest room, both drunk on perfume more viscous
than honey. Their shoes syrup-stick to the floor before
they reach your bed. They sway, sick with the brilliant scent.

iii.

Morning sickness wakes the mother, hot sleep wicking down
the hard sphere of her belly. A blue votive flame
draws her to eyes to the phone at her bedside, the number
unknown, cool voice calling for warmth just as you
signal sounds like her name in your tapering sleep.

ELDER

"quiet enough to hear the beautiful, poisoned ancestors surfacing from your diaphragm"
—Rita Wong, "reconnaissance"

all these faulty bodies
far away and constituting mine.

abuelo, healer   when I asked for teachings
I did not know I would curse you
into silence
                stroke
of unluck that undoes your voice

and I am left decaying
on the rocks   cocktail for ants
thin autumn sun bubbling
my guts out
            as I grieve
I am a ghost of the acute
light you were etched with

I dug down instead of south
and tried to winnow down
the mountains   hoping
beyond reason to emerge in yours.

now I send emissaries down
to meet an earthen belly, but

I cannot dig deep enough in time
        to bury you.

and what to do abuelo
healer   with these deaths
too far to grieve with

these   the too-far bodies
of my nearest kin

what to do abuelo
healer   to restore
your voice   your power
in the language
I have failed   to spell

the broken sigil
            of your face
            your likeness seeps
into my open mouth   a promise
a cracked tooth   a thrown set of bones

you, who knew that hauntings
            taste of rotted tongues,
will not return to teach me
more than this.

COUNTDOWN

i. 1993

I am bathing a doll in a basin
        and she shows me potted cacti,
           says never to touch their red flowers.

I am cleansing her thick, rubber skin
        for her burial.

War and cancer stumble through
this family, their clumsy movements
leaving scuff marks, leaving stones among those
overgrowths   of children like the ooze of dandelions
through the pavement.
               Mother, when you sprout me,
        your first,
                  you trace where the next stones will fall.

ii. 2003

A van packed like a tamarind pod,
hot scent of exhaust, gluey skin.
I am glommed in the backseat
with more children than seatbelts.
When our family travels together,
our safety is only in numbers.

       Abuela Islena feels carsick.
You find her an old lunchbag:
es nada, mami, ve, no huele a nada.

I breathe kid-sweat through my sleeve,
cringe away from this vomit-prone stranger.

       Years later, you tell me
her arms nursed her fourth round
of chemo when finally, visitors' visas
came through.
            Better to be revolting,
to be weak,
       than not to be remembered.

iii. 2013

You have lost count of the *cincos pa' las doce*
since she died   *en una eterna navidad.*

Those tender, chromosomal gifts
left us by *esta linda viejecita* sing in us.

      Ask: will they swell like *las campanas*
      in our bodies, as in hers.

Once, I bathed a doll
      and abuelita named the cacti
      and said never to touch their red flowers.

Once, I cleansed thick, rubber skin.

iv. 2003

Bogotá to Sudbury: 2 cents per minute.
The crackle as the calling card connects, then,
a quavering note on the phone

                                 says she has stopped.

Mother, you are far from her,

        too far away to braid your fingers
            through her   ashes
                as through hair on the head of a child
                    as her body combs into the wind.

It is a time for births and saviours,
snow-wreathed Christmas pines
and glowing, plastic front-lawn mangers.
Their blinking, artificial heat.
        I ask you if she ever touched
        the snow on the sierra while she lived.

In every church, you ask the men
to offer masses in her name,   call her to you,
but white-faced, white-haired strangers
glance away while kneeling in your pew.

Their bristling accents will not understand
             the island of her name,

                                pronounce it wrong,
      y las campanas de la iglesia están sonando,

and you shy away
from mouthing Spanish hymns
against the snow.

v. 1993

You cannot spot the freckles
that purple her hands
when you look at your own,
though their fresh root is staking
a claim on my baby-round wrists.

You fear I will not bear her gifts
with dignity, these trinkets of love
for granddaughters:

> the sepal-hued words I won't use
> her old necklace of hard leather beads
> the imminent warp of inherited skin.

vi. 2013

This, I war not to tell you.

I long for women
who taste like the skin-warmed
brass clasp of that necklace.
                              The string snaps
            when another girl's hands grasp
            my neck, its leather beads
            a rosary I count across the bed.

Girls like us betray translation.

My body instead learns
to flourish, to rush,
a live river calling out
for delicate, dowsing-rod hands.

I once bathed a doll in a basin
      while Islena showed me cacti,
      said never to touch their red flowers.

        Me voy corriendo a mi casa
        a abrazar a mi mamá.

Mother, I have hidden Islena behind
other tongues, other women.
I speak her language only
to offer its taste to a lover,
and leave none for kin.

The stones that may form in my skin
withhold my will to replicate her gifts   and yours.
Faltan cinco pa' las doce   as we count
how many minutes to the first growths.

        Mother, I will not
        give you grandchildren.

Tell me how abuela lived.
How she wore lipstick
on her last day, the sunlight
on her mouth glowing

                a shade of red unsayable
                in English. Girls like us
                betray translation.

Cuéntame.   Tell me
      we once bathed a doll in a basin
      and perfumed our wet, nylon hair
      with indelible salves.

femme phobias

The set-up is *she asked for it.*
A body rising from the water
after months unsearched-for.

If there is a straight man,
he's groping the butt
of the joke.

When you ask what she was wearing
she will cast it off, trade white cotton
for swamp-weed and nude,
bite-bruised skin, munched
by brook trout.

Wet T-shirt contest
of her decomposing chest:
you ogle as her slick moon tits
wane gibbous, pruned
and shrunken. Her cupped skin
runneth over with their bounty.

Some men don't know another way
to get a girl so wet.

She still won't smile for you.
That whore mouth, once starved
for your use is now too busy
chewing the scenery.

You always wanted her
to bring you absolution,
then dissolve.

Now her laughter
rises with her
from the water,
heralding
the flood.

Hands off, she gurgles,
and wait
for my punchline.

The advantage of a bandage
dress is all the knife wounds
you'll incur after saying "no"
in it will be pre-tourniqueted,
and still look hot.

Although—
to pull it off—
that ass is begging
to be spanxed.

Starched shirt collars
may wilt with the bus-breath
of strangers who hang
on your neckline. Work's hard,
and it's a stiff commute,
erections pressed against
your poly-blend. Just work
the rumpled look.

The parka: an all-season
rape shield. Just let them
ask, what were you wearing?
since no one's been raped
wrapped in goose down.
A good parka is water-
and-semen-resistant,
is more air-tight
than an alibi.

A push-up bra can perk up
any crowd. Full up, felt up,
feel supported
when their hands
give up the grope.

Gird your loins.
All that armour
is all that and more.

wolfwhistle—stop in your tracks
brace for impact a sidewalk assault
but no men are around and no bodies
just a window and the wolfwhistle
repeats from inside, then a squawk
not human—parrot. you can't
make this up, pretty bird pretty
bird pretty clever teach birds
not to let a bitch live. men corrupt
foul and feathered alike no sidewalk
safe but spiked tense for defense

Lately, we've scrubbed so many stains
for you, we're tinted to the eyebrows.
Our fingers match the marks you kiss
goodnight into our necks. To tuck you in
is to be drained. To drink with you
is to play oral surgery: to watch you chew
through one more wine glass, one more
dinner guest. Whose turn tonight
to hook gloved fingers, probe your mouth
for stray glass shards and strips of flesh,
whose turn to dig the grave and sink
the guest's car in the quarry, whose turn
to wrest your carcass to the shower,
where the water slices through your clothes
and through the fresh holes in your cheeks
that slowly stitch themselves, your molars
grinding all stray crumbs of glass to dust.
Let the shower's steam dissolve
all imprints of our hands on you.
Tomorrow we will wake to drink again.
Tomorrow we will call another friend
to join the whole old gang for drinks,
it's been so long. This is what you do
for family. We all bleed out together.

Fragile pink lightbulb,
skin thinner than eyelids
or crepe, I fear my teeth
will tear you, and I squint

because I've always
feared projectiles.

I'm bad at ball play.
Badminton is better;
I can watch the white web
rippling in flight, guiltless
before its impact
with my mouth.

daddy when you say you can't imagine
what two girls could do in bed
i know you mean what is *the sex*
without the p-in-v and i cannot
help feeling sorry for my mother

daddy when you say gay sex
is death-driven, i mourn
your bed death

daddy please believe me
when i tell you men are trash
since it was you who warned me
to beware of men like you

daddy never ask why girls
have called me daddy,
let me choke the words
out of our throats

daddy once you dreamed
you'd be a ballerina
and i cannot help
watching your posture
for that ghostly, graceful boy

daddy when you say the gays
are gonna kill the planet,
do you mean the aerosol emissions
of a million drag queens
aquanetting sculpted wigs

daddy when you say
i'll be the end of you
i hope you mean
the purpose

The night I heard Trixie Mattel tell a rape joke
my rapist was outed on Twitter,
& how do you follow that act.

Trixie says: I miss the days
when drag queens could be mean,
like if you left a show early, a queen
could just heckle you, something like
I hope you get raped.
& the whole room erupts.

Read me: closeted, thrift-store-leather femme
millennial, triggered & checking Twitter,
sober-slumped outside a high-school theatre
trying not to cry in front of baby gays.

Read me: stacking more triggers
than Trixie stacks wigs
when someone tweets
my rapist's name into the noise
like *what about what* _____ *did.*

Who are you,
o subtweet oracle,
to spill my filth.

Read me: still salty about Trixie
as my friends sneak selfies
at the hi-lit photobooth with her
so close behind the velvet ropes
they tell me they can smell her,

haze of hairspray, glycol mist,
& cotton candy, sweet as days
when drag shows weren't full
of women, days when gay survivors
kept the dress code: tits out,
trauma tucked. Strike
up the feminine. Punch down.
The show must glow on.

always dress for the grave-
yard's weather, that third degree
warmer than undisturbed ground.
slough another layer off
to breeze the heat, climate change
a hot, steamy affair. remember
heat is a body's last yield
unto pink wreaths of worms
that will crown hot, soft skulls.

when the vortex comes,
put down those winter whites.
lay down your cyanotic hands.
prepare your stays for their undoing.

though you knit an inch thick,
a well-dressed wreck
is all you can aspire to be.

VIRGINS

i. Je vous salue Marie

I can't knock fucking, as a Catholic—
as concept, I mean? My body is matter
for others. When he first wheedles,
can good girls *reeeeally* say no,
what he means is, can I stick it
up that schoolgirl uniform,
erotic polyester sack, ill-fitting
except where it matters. He thinks
I'm a mattress for cum stains.
When boys ask, do good girls
stay knocked up   for Jesus?
they don't mean will the uniform
stretch to fit the rise they get in us.

French Catholicism fucks me
like the plaster serpent, perfect victim,
crushed under a life-sized vierge
Marie's right foot—that statue lording
over my high school's East staircase.
Every June, the snake's anointed,
Kotex pad across the eyes, one bled on,
or painted red, who knows, to match
the lipsticked scarlet letters on the wall
spelling the names of girls who're
graduating pregnant. Just pretend
it's all immaculate conception
as a hunger eyes our tight-kneed swaths
of pantyhosed legs shushing pseudo-chastely.
There's no fucking   education here,
just abstinence from knowing
what's been done to us   already.

Le *fruit* de vos entrailles, Marie.
Are wombs so interchangeable
with entrails to you—*guts*—don't you
have a synonym to savour en prière?
Can men join in, Marie? They have
more guts than we. We've seen men
feeling up the guavas in the produce aisle
as though they're groping tits. Those fruits,
the same size as the clinic's plastic model
of the first-trimester embryo   I lost.
Marie, don't fuck around. You've seen
what men can do to girls   like us.

ii. La virgen del Carmen de Apicalá

Let us pray for my grandmother's face
when I waddle downstairs, my crotch
swaddled in wads of t.p. to ask mom
where the tampons are. Hay, madre nuestra.
Too many genitals at this family reunion,
and me too old, unmarried, due for annual
inspection. Abuela wheels to face—
not me—my mother.   ¡Pero mija!
                         ¿Niñas *virgenes*?!
and that's how goddamn Tampax
breaks my virtue seal, my best-
before-date aired out in the kitchen.

Mama laughs, at least, a perimenopausal
cackle as she lauds that modern girls
are no pale pinpricks   modern virgins
bleed pragmatically. The joke's on me.
Abuela prays at me, holding aloft
the copper icon noosed around her neck
          que nuestra virgen del Carmen
bendiga tu flor   —fucking flowers,
as though the euphemism saves me
from some phallic fold of cotton's
defloration of my sweet pedantic cunt,
or from the faltering faith of mothers
in the sacredness of girls,
                         when girls
know prayers abuela couldn't fathom.

Abuela casts only protections,
never pleasures, since mi cuerpo
es tu cuerpo   padre nuestro,
y santificados sean los hombres.
A husband is the knife you need
to justify the wound. A husband
is the prick that makes you whole.

Sometimes my Carmen is another girl,
abeula. Blood and cut. We tie our hands
together not with gold but cotton rope,
for gentleness. We weave a rhythm
like the halting lilt you pray in—
it turns out   you taught me that.

iii. Delphinapterus leucas

Scudding across the Saint Laurent
was our last date. Two horny beasts
and plus-one unicorn: M---- & C-----
& me   gone fishing, gone
whale watching. We share ice cream
on deck in steely -10, risking frostbite
or worse, observation. Tourists in Gore-Tex
crowd the railing, their matching kid sets
shrieking at our waists, the little shits.
Some tour guide crackles overhead:
belugas don't usually mate in the fall,
but let's see what's ahead, did you know
the calves drink green milk from the mothers?

The tugboat sidles to a white knot,
a disturbance   sound of water,
of whales, which is mostly more water,
more roiling whales than we can count,
dozens. So much muscle brawning
at the surface.   Slick white skin,
like clotted paint, says C-----,
and M---- confirms it's eggshell.
Some kid shouting: mom mom
are they fighting   what's that
red thing   does that hurt?

So many long, maroon harpoons
bob in the water. They nod fiercely,
wield hunger too sore to explain
as they slip-slide, leave score marks
on white rubber flanks. Science knows
so little of beluga sex. They've made
the Wikipedia list of homosexual species.
No list mentions the orgies, but we know
belugas only mate with full consent,
a pearly underwater dance.   Science

could learn a thing or two. We three
tongue at a slurry of whale-white ice
cream   vanilla? We take turns,
slurping liquefied forms of the haloes
we've lost. Tonight, our naked arms
will crackle together like radio static,
transmitting dead voices in prayer
from my asthmatic youth. Look how far
we come   for sweetness in the cold.

doppelbanger

Our marooned armchairs are overripe. Split-
plum upholstery. The buttons sinking into juicy folds.

Emmett says he's sensual, a really nice sponge.
Scrubs the age-rings from cross-sectioned coral.

Driving in, he says, he caught a flash of Sasquatch
masturbating in a church of poison oak.

Nab a snatch of romance as you pass: her bouquet
of wagging pistils, her elastic, tooth-marked garter.

Overheard: "Pussycat Dolls played at my high school!"
Overheard: "It wasn't pleasure, it was routine."

UNDERBELLY

When the blood is cut with acid rain,
all touch pollutes. Lips to brow.

Oversaturated silt will oxidize its waters
and leave ore deposits blinking up, glaucomatous.

Pour my molten afterbirth down the black hills.
Watch the drip trails reach out: burning, liquefied limbs.

I am mourning my pubescent faith
that all things come to flower.

Months ago, I shed my ilia on your front porch.
Return my bones before raccoons scavenge my sex.

Kitchens are complex turn-ons. I peel off my unmentionable
past, domestic shame. Papaya simmers to candy on the stove.

Parlour trick: you flush rose quartz
and crystallize: gem-cut bust on the plinth of your chest.

I'm the cool tourniquet of the garter
snake coiling around your left thigh.

We take comfort in clichés of heart and hearth,
in the colour of blown coals, blown fuses.

We met in a shamefully hot game of Twister,
the carpet a marshland that doused us with swamp gas.

DEMI-CLOS

My ear canals are tightly corseted hysterics.
Heed the wet pop when they can't take the pressure.

I keep all my unborn babies
in the hollows of my cyanide-capsule teeth.

A rugged cock's comb of conch at your bedside
siphons wet dreams from your skull.

Peonies erupt in the village: swollen
heads, facefulls of bee-sting.

When crossing the road, look at the boy's face,
not the spray of his skull over stone.

BEDROOM SCENE

Pinpricks in the vinyl blackout blinds.
You've needled glory holes for Cassiopeia's stars.

Impossible animals sinew the crane of your bent neck.
The hunch of a deaf unicorn. The antler-bowed brow of a dove.

Guessing your feelings is like charming a cobra
with a stethoscope. My only rhythm is a tachycardic reel.

O my little blue loon,
let us meet again soon.

You can't reach your pants; the swans
at my bedside are pecking your pockets to bits.

OH, BABY

Mid-flight turbulence. The Dash-8 seatbelt
lashed over your pelvis. This thrill of constriction.

We want thunder for the squalling child
and ivies coiling closer to the windows of the sickly.

The falling arches of cathedrals, of my instep.
This body's architecture cannot bear your weight.

You know, I couldn't unmolest
my childhood if I tried.

We can hoist our sins over the rails,
but the stroller will always be with us.

Wanting you is like waiting for lightning
to strike me each time I smell rain.

The heat stings your skin in sharp swifts,
a spiked roller of dressmaker's pins.

Come fix me with your pearl eyes
in the wildflowers by the road.

Traces of shell, manure, earth. Rake
the flesh and prepare for a harvest of salt.

The hacked geometry of granite bluffs hatched
across your back. We press you close until it cuts.

IT'S A GIVEN

Black spruce swoop at oil-clots of swamp,
crack their spines to wing-tip foul water.

The thunder of felled pines maelstroms
as it sounds the lake bottom for bodies.

Stroking my ponyhair shoes, I commune
with the dead horse who gave me his hide.

You glaze a funeral pyre with jack pine sap.
You extend a hand scarred from charred bark.

The flocked froth of lily pads, brushed,
is velour to the touch. We'll pay dearly for this.

When the maelstrom swallows up the coast,
race for the food trucks, one last Fredericton samosa.

You'll find your teenager gets off to vintage Harry Potter slash.
You'll remember the saga you blogged at their age, and get sweaty.

All-you-can-eat *sopa de tripa*. Bowl after bowl, you slide your tongue
over boiled, well-spiced villi. The rogue texture of rumen, smooth omasum.

Overheard: "I hope it's not, like, super spiritual in India, cuz I want,
like, lots of malls to be open. Like, it takes guts, to travel alone, yeah?"

You will not jump off the springboard. You foresee the blade
of water surging trenchant through the soft coves in your thorax.

RESIDUAL

The mark left by a blackbird, hit at highway speed:
a trace of cartilage, a shard of hollow wing-bone.

Use birch skin for papier-mâché,
for taxidermic salves, for origami getaway sedans.

They changed the timbre of the streetlights,
but the nights still taste of whiskeyed, brassy orbs.

Shedding your hair like chaff, bare scalp rebaptized
by the north wind. Shitty harvest this year, ain't it?

Omission is no sin. I fold the socks you left
into a talisman I'll water in the window-box for blooms.

CRYPTOECOLOGY

Our shores shrink with the mercury. We gain density,
shed members: you glide legless, and I'm greying at the hands.

There are no borders in a lake zone, only tailings pond,
cool spring, and brook-trout semen melding underground.

We're ailed with vapours: the spit of wet oak,
and the black fever sprung from our brows.

The rust pulse of a sliced thumb in the mouth mimics
the beat of falling rain, its metallic gush oiling your chin.

Lakes gather teeth from dead walleye, lost swimmers,
and rumoured cetaceans. Keep clear of islands' jawlines.

TACTILES

Dusk leaves circle your feet, and damp moths
waft wingbeats of mushroom, hay, myrrh.

I smell the slight on you: hot, astringent
from the furred snouts of your coat sleeves.

A malignant growth of poppies darts pins
at the chanting breasts of children.

Window-sweat embalms a mosquito you crushed.
Our two bloods mingle, unravel like artificial silk.

Between highway pines, white eyes gather
like lint, fray on bare bracken spires.

Peer through plumes of steam for tea-leaf omens.
They stare back, indignant. Prophecies need privacy.

The glass face atop the mantle sweats with shame,
your nude reflection warping in its cheek.

Your pupils dilate when the portrait hung
over the bed winks, its aperture irises flashing.

See me pulling small fish from my skin.
Their excision is ecstasy.

Those molars stashed in vintage pewter snuffboxes
are chattering. They know the things you do.

My daughters still chew their fingernails. I see where their enamel
is chipped when they come pour my tonics for me.

There's a reason you can only write beginnings, plagued
as you are by those torturous visions no glass can correct.

It goes without saying: that thing we did not do last week
is behind the grey file cabinet this grey morning.

It's all slander and lies, salamanders and lye,
salmonella and limes, salvaged divorcée lust, you and I.

A rhetoric of fear is graffitied all over the walls. He says,
"I've got a *nasty* dynasty going on here."

Low, rose moon, let us pray for the sadsaps among us.
One more slump, and the maple tide sours before tapping.

I'm hung up on another missed phone call. Warn me
next time yesterday's tomorrow doesn't mean tonight.

Little thief, little gleaners: the dust mites, the dry condom
stashed in the pink afghan sheathing my childhood bed.

Like a split trunk standing after the clear-cut,
I can't fail to get the short end of your schtick.

My proclivity for groping, for squeezing
the cacti. Needles to say, self-love stings.

TRYPOPHOBIA

After a rash of cabin fever, dark splatter
marks the pocked flank of a snowbank.

This town is riddled with desire
paths, wormed through with warmth.

I try to find relief in the topography
of gooseflesh I raise across your back.

A flourish of tongue-thick petals.
The corpse-flower's beetroot and puce hues.

Clouds swell with copper bruises on their bellies
where the smelter fires press against the night.

Proving punk lives on underwater, soda tabs jangle
from the lips of rainbow trout and strung-out morays.

If there's any style running through the new apartment,
it's roach. Redecorate with terra cotta vases, sprigs of bay leaf.

I'm gargoyle-perched to watch the first snow fall.
My haggard, leathern wings will keep me warm.

The lost limb of the doll you're reassembling
suntans on the plastic island scumming the Atlantic.

Here fly the herons of apocalypse, the cormorants
of rainswept armies, and the mallards of the flood.

MISS

My doppelganger's crying in her sleep again.
She can't be both care giver and care taker.

Yoga warms us up to sink down and complete
the primal keening: pigeon, cat, hound, corpse.

My lacklustre séance summons just
a jaundiced flicker of your form.

Shedding a reject selfie of its cleavage, the cervix
casts a narcissistic portrait of its sex.

Chihuahuas' faces wear their foretold deaths,
and Pomeranians pant your next memento mori.

The skunk prefers to flee than to attack. It knows how bees
fear stinging for the way the act extracts their creamy innards.

When the wind mouths abandoned church bells, it sucks
dry lips over their hollows, binding their tongues.

Be gentle with the lake surface. Its fresh veil of ice is
a bedsheet pulled taut, puckered over the corners.

Your hands gripping my throat cannot silence the pulse
of a vein throbbing my growled contralto.

Bare feet skirt bathroom tile at three a.m. You move like the fish
you once squeezed while withdrawing a hook from its jaw.

SOOTHSAYER

The gothic boom: a dog's bark peals downwind
and peels a layer from a maple sapling's skin.

Sleep is a brush with which we scorn
to sweep our loam-caked fingernails.

Stop and smell the lichens. Breathe the factory-
fume-infused fug of the parched fire moss.

I used to be an irritant, a braggart,
but all my overreactions were anaphylactic.

On northern highways, keep a mourning dove above
in case your windshield faceplants in the fireweeds.

After pausing to rest your good leg below the granaries,
you answered me by trickling away into wheat germ.

We hope we don't smell like our lust, though we bundle it
under our pillows, and bathe in its castles by night.

Proximity and plenitude are queasy lovers,
too young, still, to move with ease in tandem.

Don't tell me it's precision that I lack. Lean closer
and my crooked nose will cut a bitch.

If my arm hair grows in blonde
I will be ready to be loved.

BODY HEAT

The glitter outline of your torso on the bed confesses
that we cannot guess what marks we make.

Skin like the surface of the sun. Any touch encroaching
on your orbit burns to ash, neglects to scar.

My food addiction when your pregnancy end-stopped.
I gained your baby-weight. *I didn't know if this was empathy or theft.*

Mommy look I am drawing you mommy
it looks just like you look and you have no face.

Since the fire boiled the fat from my bones, I'm a billowing tarp
at half-mast on the scaffolding. Watch me swell in the updraft.

Never early to rise, you were early to leave things
unsaid. If you want to be haunting, stop ghosting.

Two wheelchairs pilfered from the psych ward are abandoned
In the parking lot. Wind-rocked, like porch swings.

Even fallen women must remind men
our eyes are down here.

A thimble of blue hemoglobin serum
where blood-drops pulse like smoke rings.

You can disappoint me any time.
I know, duty is only sin-deep.

MISS

My doppelganger's crying in her sleep again.
For all our co-dependence, we are paying twice the price.

If I'm just a young bitch, watch me do young bitch things:
whimper-text my ex, pitch my poor self-worth to his command.

I carry you, love, to the slab. I vacuum
your lungs through your spatchcocked arm sockets.

That flaccid crook of shoulder in the toilet.
That mottled blot of flesh my nearest kin.

Heave your axe at the oak of our overnights.
Go on. Have one more dusky go at my stumps.

LOVEY-DOVEY

First memory: sunrise seeps through pressed hands.
The salt smell and blood-orange light.

You're my Brooklyn jazz cellist,
my barefoot, dog-walking cartographer.

When I pine for you, I burn
perfumed with gum and resin.

You would trek across town with your face
peeling off, it's so cold, just to warm me.

You are oversized, rose-tinted glasses.
I ache only to love everything.

REASONABLE GROUND

With all our ups and downs, at what point
does our inclination lead to our decline?

For failed object permanence, please press one. For jealousy,
press three. For polyamory, press any number, gently.

Let us drink, let us pool in our cupped palms
my sexual traumas, your chain-smoked monogamies.

I have been missing your voice
like bleached bones dream of flesh.

We are both anxious cancers just waiting to happen.
Come, let us probe one another for overgrowths.

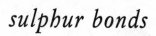

sulphur bonds

ACID RAIN

it's like we cannot get this place
out of our systems, like we cannot
neutralize our caustic origins.

PH imbalance in my dry mouth,
spit like CLR. my nostrils crack
and bleed. my wetness bleaches
underwear, makes long white eyes
that stare unblinking into me.

do you feel it too, old love,
the boil and bubble in your gut?

my body is hyperreactive,
sharp sulphuric medium
hostile to most life forms.
trust me—i tried every cure,
every quick-lime and cleanse.
it resists bicarbonates, magnesia
wash, raw detox diets, soft ash
scattered across my forest beds.

i have curdled every future,
every embryo that enters me.
i am a mass of suicidal proteins
in hydrolysis, denaturing, entropic.

my desire to heal is just a thermic burn,
release of peptide bonds as i dissolve.
if my lovers or my engineers since you
have felt my warmth, it was no love—

how could acidic bodies like our own
even begin to breed a future.

and who can we blame for the times
we made out by the tailings ponds,
enraptured by their iridescent blue, lusting
to get a life upon these rain-burned rocks.

BIG NICKEL MINE ROAD

so preoccupied
with my own
displacement
didn't notice
i was displacing

you

—Vivek Shraya "amiskwacîwâskahikan"

the screel of night trains carting hydrofluoric acid
through a nyquil-drowsy suburb // notice how
this road bypasses every issue, each emission
of the sulphur-gushing mines // bet heads or tails,
& scowl back at the king on the big nickel,
coarse colonial frown & dour brow dagger-eyeing
down the highway at a residential school
dry-husked since 1965

                     // learning english,
brown immigrant child thrilled with hope
by a map-spot marked spanish, ontario,
maybe-haven where she might be understood
that is instead a haunting of other brown faces,
other mother tongues excised //

                     since 1948
across the crater valley, propped against slag
hills (white) schools for (white) settler children
teach (white) official languages, decry assimilation
of (white) francophones by (white) anglophones,
& mobilize the land's (white) history

                                        // what words,
if any, do we brown ghosts share for losses
we are not allowed to grieve, what ceremony can i offer
when my spells are just another colonizer's tongue,
a (foreign) language of forgetting //

                                history buried
so close you cannot tell its warmth from sunlight,
feel it radiating daily // notice how this road bypasses
every issue, how i cannot drive this story
sans collision // look for dripping irony,
i mean, for iron ore molten & luminous
& oozing down the slag heaps from thick crucibles
the size of fishing huts & sink together through lake ice
& hear the huts gulp, punctured drums // & taste
the run-off, acid-green and viscous in the snow

anchor babies implant families in the soft white folds called north
america / no middle names because my parents thought canadians don't
gift their offspring litanies of generations / I am the gift they provide to
belong /

in mining towns tensions and pensions are highest since few
live too long and why not bribe the ones who must die, silicosis and
cancer the severance / my parents never venture underground and have
no pensions, too preoccupied with surfaces / architect, healer / those
foreign degrees deemed contaminants to the white ore /

this crater
town a pool of heavy metals, ozone gas, sulphur dioxide / my
parents wear their cancer genes and wade into elusive promises / all
I learn about bodies is abstinence only, until implantation or death /
little immigrant girls learn bilingual baby names before they learn to
bleed /

what nature / what nurture will I replicate if ever I can birth
a living child / what thing must I become to mother the misshapen
clod of tissue, muscle, teeth my body wrecks / *I am a minus producing
machine* /

what chimera of accumulated toxins and forced faith makes a
legacy / little immigrant girls learn that childless desire pollutes true
patriot hearts / every body will bear so much unselflike matter / every
body will die, it's the only sustainable burden

COMMUTE QUARTET

i.

A woman carries motionless, white wolves
under her arms, woven into the fleece
of her jacket. November, no shoes,
and the song she hums low to her wolves
burns as fierce overhead as a sermon.

ii.

Doubled over in the threshold of the building
marked "For Lease" to fix the ankle-straps
of platformed, gold-foil sandals. The crackling
shimmer of her neon turquoise tracksuit
is a time machine waiting to happen.

iii.

She shows only the back of her head, claims
three seats at the front of the bus. Her face
cloaked by hair pushed forward, grey encrypted
in its coarse, black strands. She beats her feet
in Morse code on the floor, dares all to read.

iv.

A pristine grease mark on a window spells
a soft pattern of curls like the scraps
of a decomposed love letter buried for years.
Peer through the soggy resolve of the marks
that remain to see what was smudged out.

301 Lasalle / Madison

Leaves leaving scorch marks over sidewalks,
last warmth fondling the sleeves of young girls'
winter coats, those coats that smell of naphthalene
and coconut hair glitter after aestivating in warm closets.
North wind snuffling their coat hems like the puppy
always nosing strangers' crotches. You and I part ways
downtown, brush ungloved hands. This is how to leave
a body as the bus huffs onto Elm, then hoists its hulk out
kitty-corner to where Paris genuflects to Notre Dame.
I chuff through the Moulin à fleur 20 km over the limit.
The woman in the seat in front of mine a bloomless droop,
the tulip stalk you swore you'd clear in August. Her arm
bouncing accusingly. When traffic cuts to red, I levitate,
and her head hits the window. This is how you leave
a body be. A languid baritone hums underneath the cut-
down bells of St. Jean de Brébeuf. As they sink
there is warmth in their patina'd domes, where the snow
will not fall, but where after-church bickering funnels
and smoulders to ash. You said this town lacked mystery,
but the bus looms past the silos, those chopped rounds
of elephant birches. Their silent but tangible trumpeting,
those nose-blows, all to puff out the sulphur dioxide fumes
tarnishing them. The banality of evil is that poltergeists
are bad for traffic. The tulip woman curls her arm
to halo safe her baby, who blabs in reply to those moans
as we careen over the lurching tracks at Wilma Street.
His mother coils her halo closer yet to wreath his toqued
head from colliding with the greased glass of the window.
His toque is the colour of the first winters witnessed

by nonagenarians who now count the cars from their windows
in Pioneer Manor, the colour of the yarns
that they spin to different nurses every morning. Snagged
by the gravity that pulls towards Val Caron, the bus struggles
to merge onto Lasalle, where dusk congeals the traffic
to a mournful drawl. This is how to hold your breath
passing the graveyard at a traffic crawl. Squint for names
before the night-frost glazes out the dates pressed shallow
in stone markers. Frost comes so soon, no time for summer
flesh to cool, coagulate, no time for baby's-breath-swathed
yellow roses on the graves to try to breed with spirited
exhalations from below the hardened clay. You don't know
I once bunny-hopped gravestones to make out with Jorge.
He led me to the old dam where the low-rent graves grin
thick with teen graffiti. When I stumbled, it was on a weedy
granite flat that bore your mother's father's name. Poppy
and dandelion browning from his gut. This was how I left
my body: in sandy boy-hands. The sound of keening scrapes
the bus, and not the baby's, though his wet clay
hands cast out for balance. It's the man weeping his spleen
into an empty seat. But you never liked sentiment,
did you? The sidewalks heave around Félix-Ricard,
swollen with early trick-or-treaters. Matted plush lions,
crepe firemen with candy-slicked mouths. Pain
is just a choking hazard in a too-small throat.
Candy too likely laced with old razors to swallow.

At one forty-eight, the driver unlocks the one-thirty bus.
You board, an alphabetical procession of iron-on flags:
Brazil and Colombia on backpacks, then Denmark, Italy,
Ukraine, on trucker caps. A ceremonial FIFA cast-off
défilage, the colours merging in the monochrome
of strained fluorescent lighting as the bus roars.
You're washed the hue of no-name window cleaner.
Dregs in age-old plastic bottles in the side sheds
and garages that are cluttered past downtown. Whole city
poking through its jars of odd nails, airing out the wrinkles
of those neighbourhoods which, folded up for winter,
gather grime and hair and brown-black beetle shells,
turn stiff as dish-rags. Hard creases like the hyphenate-
Canadians in the bus, crusted a little with hard water.
Individual names scurry like dogs hiding from vacuums,
panting safe behind the couch. Peer while passing black
and ochre snowbanks coating hills near the Caruso Club,
where neat crostoli houses shed white paint, chipping
their powdered-sugar frostings. Late Christmas boughs
still wreath their doors. Odd neighbours keeping up
with the Giovannis still boast plastic Hallowe'en-bag
witches, stretching sodden grins across the re-thawed
lawns. The bus scours the curb, turning corners.
It's a day for scouring sidewalk salt off the dog's paws.
Someone on Gilmore Avenue scours the AM off
a parked BULANCE. It's a safer neighbourhood since
Vale decked the slag heaps out in sod. Now, kinder
shadows overcast the bypass, looming dark and whalish
from the bypass, sloughing snow off like innocent hills.
They've acquired a lazy fringe across their tops of bony,
adolescent birches. Like the mines are winking sleepily
over St. Anthony's on Mary Street. The smokestack

yawning limpid, ashy-peach smoke at the snow. Smell
its rusty breath as the bus rattles off the 55 onto Balsam,
where the Copper Cliffers, deaf to the tremor of blasting,
putter in stout brick churches and in warped, basementless
houses built quick for the miners in olde boom years.
The turn onto Serpentine shakes loose the smells
that have burrowed in the balding plush bus seats:
white onion fried in peanut oil, an empty paper bag
now oozing grease onto an empty seat, the warmth of bread
perpetually baking at the factory on Lorne. That early litany
of flags trickled away somewhere on Gutcher, wondering
what cruel butcher named that street. Who named Diorite,
too, the bus climbing its rucked back into Littler Italy,
where houses huddle closer from the falling price of nickel.
Alight on the rock. Metallic razor of the wind scouring
the peach hairs from your face. The bus rattles, arthritic,
back through overgrowths of plywood home extensions
insulated by the snowbanks. Turn, and feel the creases
multiplying in your neck, sculpting the pattern
of these narrow, winding lanes as you crane upwards,
point your chin towards the blind mouth of the smokestack
and let its vertiginous form bow its lips to meet yours.

Washed ashore,
my once indigo paint
has been ghosted and sapped
to the pallor of uncooked
chicken breasts. Preternaturally
copper-green, the water suffers
barren poplar branches to gouge
through my calcified flesh
as they ripple and leer.
Acid snowmelts eroded
my sight. I keep company
only with stones whose ores
miscarried them under
this glass-dark surface.
Here, our memories reflect
how, that summer,
she threw me away
from between her knees,
forgetting where I fell
once the blood was staunched,
once the cold gelled me below.

CONTACT DERMATITIS

as we name the pollutants
that spool out from the mines,
contour the lines around my eyes:
erosion tracks, skin fizzed away
by irritant and rash. highlight
my rare venetian mask,
this face untreatable,
precambrian shield furrowed
by acid rain. fan-brush
my chronic itch with shimmer.
beautify my trace deposits.

and how to trace this ancestry
except by what is done to me
to make my skin consumable:

café au lait. light cocoa.
butterscotch. brown sugar.
cinnamon. warm toast.
old sand. ash grey.
shit brown.
darky.
ugly spic.

brown is the itch unnameable.
crass palimpsest of origins
obscured by migrant love,
colonial hell, a violent
complexion freckling my nose.

what's dirtier: my dna,
a lead-based powder,
or the toxic soil i root in.

glitter me with fine-ground mica,
that breakable flaw in the rock,
that mineral shot through with mirrors.

my skin is riddled
with acceptance, pores
burnt open to admit.

who knew rocks are not whalebacks
slicked black cresting from acid
residue corrosion when I left Sudbury
the limestone cliffs of Manitoulin
gleamed cream and unpolluted to the eye

this ugly whitegirl knew more kinship
from the black rock against her brown skin
than from you we both were tainted
our complexions shamebrands of pollution

there are mornings when the smokestack
windless veils itself in sulphur to seduce
itself into my old backyard remember
not in your backyard as though your white-
washed picket fences hold back SO$_2$

who knew whiteness was no guarantee
of purity who knew my openness
to sunlight was what made me violable
as though you too are not an opening
as though whiteness reflects deflects
any incursion of water bacterium rust

who knew the ivory tower I climbed
to lift my head above the smoke
that con of godliness that only beacon
of respectability for immigrant children
spews acid enough carves a brace of blades
aimed towards this toodark flesh
awaiting any movement for the pleasure
of a passive cut, the gloried stance of blame

the cancers we cut from our loved ones
outnumber us on certain streets each home
proffers metastasis in every clench of blasting
underfoot in every home garden tomato
in every touch on the brow who thought
I'd miss my second mother's last days
living the sweat of her third cancer

who knew her white body could harbour
the uncleanness my dark skin attests to
could we have lived to bathe together
make ablutions of our mutual corruption
or could we find a stream where water runs
unglittered by a thick mantle of nickel

This is not about the whiteness
of metal raised up from below.
What violence is done to you
on your behalf? This poem
is not about race, but the race
to mine nickel, white gold.
Mind your head down here,
it's sticks holding up stones
and which breaks first?
       Skip it: how-ma-ny-mine-shafts
       have-col-lapsed? Echolocate
       the soft pockets in rockfall
       where bodies of ghost miners
       decompose, greasing the rock
       with their fat, a subterranean
       anointment. This is sainthood.
       Revelation. This is canonization.
           The pop-pop-pop-crumble
           of dynamite blasts is the cough
           of a non-human god, is a phlegm
           benediction, god's last breath
           a boom. Here lie immigrant
           ghost men in rubble. Their trouble:
           to garnish white women
           with nickel-free pendants
           and chains.
               What violence
                   is done to you?

This poem is not
about race. Ignore the pumice stones
we grind into our skin, exfoliating
brown for bone. Squeezing blood
from the rock is self-mortification.
This old ghost town is hollow:
3500 km of roads built over
5000 km of tunnel, runnel, shaft.

This infrastructure runs chthonic.
Erosion means: when-will-the sink-
hole-swal-low-you? My underworld
is richer than your underworld
and lighter-skinned. When white
metal extracted and stacked
aboveground weighs its options,
it will take the landslide victory.

The town smells like a yuppie garbage day,
artisanal and yeasty. It pairs well
with the basement wine that coats
your throat: acidic, glutinous, and wistful.

You weave a chain of rusty daisies
at the playground near the creek
clogged with fluorescent silt. Inhale
the sulphurous tang it belches up.

The lightness of your swiss-cheese bones
is not enough to fly, not yet. Both sourdough
and cancer stats are rising in this kitchen.

I spill tea over yesterday's stale crumbs.
We watch them swell like lymphocytes
and read in them the pattern of our likeness.

Pray with me: recite the names of lakes
from which our tap water is drawn.

We drive past rolling shattercones
while you try not to fracture. Rain
here corrodes the edges of your car,
corrodes the edges of your patience.

As a bone-witch, I'm no use to you.
Bones that may shift under my hands
do not regain their lost opacity.

I couldn't even heal myself, dashing
my elbows on the rocks to cleanse
us all of what has seeped in through our skin.

We make such solipsisms on these rare,
hop-seasoned nights. We swaddle newborn
lambs and nurse them from our bottles,
curse their innocence, their tabula rasa

immune systems. Tipsy nurturers, we tally
parts per million nickeling their bloodstreams
as they grow. We can't be healed of love

for landscapes. Let's drink until my drunk body
mistakes home for poison, closes up my throat.
Let's drink until your body overgrows this place.

In "Colombiana," the line "this B-movie blast of bloody blam blam" is from Betsy Sharkey's review of the 2011 film *Colombiana*, in *The Los Angeles Times*.

The epigraph to "Elder" is from Rita Wong's "reconnaissance" in *Forage*.

The italicized lines in "Countdown" are from Néstor Zavarce's song, "Faltan cinco pa' las doce."

"Outings" references a performance by Trixie Mattel given in K'jipuktuk, Mi'kmaq territory, in January, 2018.

The italicized lines in "Body heat" and "Bedroom scene" are from Leslie Jamison's *The Empathy Exams*.

The epigraph to "Big Nickel Mine Road" is from Vivek Shraya's "amisk-wacîwâskahikan" in *even this page is white*.

The italicized line in "child / machine" is from Kim Hyesoon's "Morning Greetings" in *Sorrowtoothpaste Mirrorcream*, as translated by Don Mee Choi.

ACKNOWLEDGEMENTS

Deepest thanks to editor Dionne Brand, for seeing a burning thing and stoking it. Thanks to Kelly Joseph and the M&S poetry team for guiding this book into existence, to the Canada Council for the Arts for financial support, and to Canisia Lubrin, without whom this book would not have found a home.

Thanks to the editors of the magazines and anthologies in which some of these poems or their previous incarnations appear: *Arc; Cosmonauts Avenue; CV2; Dusie; The Hart House Review; Lemon Hound; The Malahat Review; Minola Review; Poemeleon; PRISM International; The Puritan; Room; terra north/nord; Gush: Menstrual Manifestos of Our Times;* and *Another Dysfunctional Cancer Poem Anthology.* Thanks to the chapbook editors at Anstruther Press and Rahila's Ghost, who raised these poems to their full voice.

To my post-CO luvs: Alicia Elliott, Carrianne Leung, Cason Sharpe, Eli Tareq Lynch, Jenny Heijun Wills, Kim Senklip Harvey, Leonarda Carranza, Minelle Mahtani, Natalie Wee, Prathna Lor, Whitney French, and Canisia Lubrin—your writing, spirits, and support are making futures we can thrive in.

Ever thanks to Emily Skov-Nielsen and Katie Fewster-Yan for our poetry covens and cosmic friendship. To Claire Kelly, Rob Ross, and Michael Meagher for wisdom and poetry sandwiches. To Ross Leckie for embracing storytelling at its fullest. To Triny Finlay, who helped me to rebuild these poems in their worst year. To Lisa Banks and Patrick O'Reilly for unfailingly magical kindness. To Lauren Korn and C.L. Johnson for writing poems that gently break open. To Lauren Turner for sharing survival poetics. To Brendan Vidito, for the earliest of writing friendships. And to Melanie Durette, who told me to never stop writing, long before I needed to hear it.

Lastly, gracias a mis familias of origin and choice. A los Salazar y los Leon que animan mi voz, y todos que llenan mi vida—Paco, Javier, Patricia, Heath, Maggie, Siobhan, Duncan, Amber, Indigo, and all those we have loved. Our stories are fluid and changing, but never less true.

© Sam Evans

REBECCA SALAZAR (she/they) is a writer, editor, and community orga-
nizer currently living on the unceded territory of the Wolastoqiyik
people. The author of poetry chapbooks *the knife you need to justify the
wound* (Rahila's Ghost) and *Guzzle* (Anstruther), Salazar also edits for
The Fiddlehead and *Plenitude* magazines.